THE CLASSIC ROCK PHOTOS OF BARON WOLMAN
MY GENERATION
INSTAGRAM POSTINGS OF *ROLLING STONE'S* FIRST PHOTOGRAPHER

THE CLASSIC ROCK PHOTOS OF BARON WOLMAN

MY GENERATION

INSTAGRAM POSTINGS OF *ROLLING STONE'S* FIRST PHOTOGRAPHER

OMNIBUS PRESS

London / New York / Paris / Sydney / Copenhagen / Berlin / Madrid / Tokyo

ROLLING STONE

November 20, 1967
Vol. 1, No. 2
OUR PRICE: TWENTY-FIVE CENTS

TINA TURNER SOCKIN' IT TO YOU—See Page Two

Bob Dylan Alive in Nashville; Work Starts On New LP

A bearded Bob Dylan is alive, well, and recording in Nashville, having finally emerged from his retreat in Woodstock, New York.

In the first two sessions at Columbia's country and western studios, in Nashville, Tennessee, Dylan has recorded three songs: "The Drifter's Escape" is Kafkaesque tale about a man on trial for nothing; "I Dreamed I Saw St. Augustine," and "Frankie Lee and Julias Priest." The first two are between three and four minutes long, and the last just over five and a half minutes.

An authoritative source says the feeling of the songs is close to that of Highway 61 Revisited. Dylan's voice has a fuller sound, says the source, and he is trying to "sing" the tracks, not to chant or talk the lyrics. All are done in a middle tempo, and the backing musicians are all from Nashville.

Producer Bob Johnston, who did Blonde on Blonde, and Highway 61 is pleased with the work so far, as are Columbia executives who have set no release date but want the album out as quickly as possible.

A session last week was planned to complete the album. Columbia has other Dylan songs in the can, but since he is back actively writing and recording, it is every doubtful that they will be released.

Lester Flatt and Earl Scruggs will soon be releasing "Top of the Flood," a song Bob wrote recently especially for the bluegrass group.

No one but musicians and technicians have been allowed into the studio, but Dylan has been seen in public in Nashville. The beard is a chin and jaw line bush that makes him look like Abraham Lincoln, particularly since his hair is shorter and he is sporting a black, Mennolite-style hat. He looks well, say those who have seen him, and his motorcycle accident in August, 1966, has left no visible scars or other damage, as was rumored in the press.

IN THIS ISSUE:

JEFFERSON AIRPLANE: Marty Balin talks about the group's new album . . . . . . Page 4

McNEAR'S BEACH: Big Brother and the Holding Company at an outdoor benefit — a photo-feature . . . . . . Page 10

DONOVAN: Part two of the Rolling Stone interview — the Maharishi, Gypsy Dave and Donovan's new film . . . . . . Page 12

ROLLING STONE

ACME   FEBRUARY 1, 1969   No. 26   UK: 3/6   35 CENTS

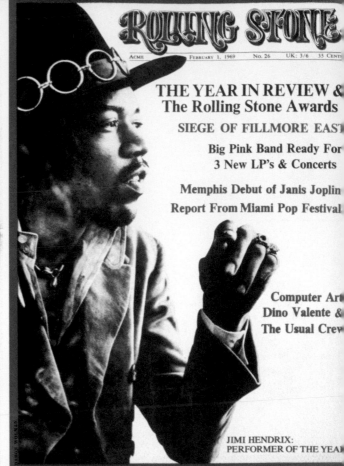

THE YEAR IN REVIEW & The Rolling Stone Awards

SIEGE OF FILLMORE EAST

Big Pink Band Ready For 3 New LP's & Concerts

Memphis Debut of Janis Joplin

Report From Miami Pop Festival

Computer Art
Dino Valente &
The Usual Crew

JIMI HENDRIX: PERFORMER OF THE YEAR

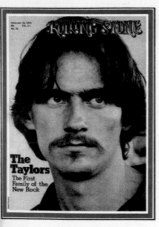

The Taylors
The First Family of the New Rock

ROLLING STONE

ACME   JULY 26, 1969   Twenty-five cents

This Issue
...'s New Record Bombed
...Stone Interview
...Frank Zappa

Dylan in the Studio With George

Paul Simon, If Anybody Asks

Little Richard Child of God

Janis Back From Jungle!

Cream's Last Puff

ROLLING STONE

May 28, 1968   Twenty-five cents

New Beatles Album: Ringo Snubs Queen
$50,000 Missing in Monterey . . . Bob Dylan's Nashville

The Beatles May Do Free Spring Concert Tour in U.S.A.

Tribute to the Lone Star State:

DISPOSSESSED MEN AND MOTHERS OF TEXAS

THE NEW JOAN BAEZ, A LITTLE OLDER NOW

Norman Mailer
Carl Perkins
Jimi Hendrix
Felix Paparelli
& Others

ROLLING STONE ROLLING STONE

get it here

THE DOPE CRISIS

GOOD OLD GRATEFUL DEAD

ROLLING STONE

ACME   No. 60   August 23, 1968   UK: 2/6   75 Cents

A Special Super-Duper Neat Issue:

ROLLING STONE

The GROUPIES and Other Girls

ANNA

~~TRIKE MERKIN~~

The GTO's

THE PLASTER CASTERS

Foreword

SINCE ITS LAUNCH in October, 2010, Instagram has become the world's visual lingua franca, one of the most popular methods of communication among the peoples of our planet. Instagram has 500 million daily users and I'm one of them. You might even say I have become addicted to Instagram. For the most part it's a 'responsible' addiction, especially since photos have long been my primary language. Although statistically unconfirmed, it seems to be the case that these days people, particularly the young, are 'talking' among themselves with pictures rather than with words. I prefer a blend of the two, which is how I compose my own Instagram posts, understanding that words are not entirely necessary since the best pictures tell their own full stories.

I have discovered some extraordinarily talented and inspirational artists on Instagram, often following labyrinthine links from one person to another, noting who they follow. Instagram is also a window into the worlds of others – where else can we learn so much about the interests of friends and families or the art that comprises the lives of our fellow travelers. Some say we're only seeing the universe that people choose to present, a sanitized version of their own lives. Some say there is a whole lot of narcissism happening on Instagram. To some degree both are true, yet for me peering through its cyber window is an endless delight, occupying decidedly too much of my free time.

Meanwhile, looking back at my music pictures, as well as those of my contemporaries, I'm also finding that there is something different about music photography today. Maybe it's the predominance of color, maybe it's the technical excellence of the photographic equipment (mostly digital), of the images, and of the shooters themselves. Back in my day, of course, there was no auto-focus, no auto-exposure and definitely no digital. I'm not complaining, simply stating the obvious, articulating thoughts that occur to me as I visit Instagram and enjoy the work of today's music photographers. Many use hi-tech Nikons and Canons, or even iPhones, and most clearly love music and musicians, which is no doubt why they share photos with their followers. There are a few music shooters I greatly admire, both men and women who are making captivating photos and posting them on Instagram, confirming their dedication to the subject and their craft.

I had the benefit of all areas access; I could go anywhere with my cameras, range the music landscape far and wide, be anywhere an image was waiting to be captured. I also had the singular benefit of working with *Rolling Stone* magazine, which, at the time, was the only game in town for musicians who wanted to be seen by their fans. The musicians needed us to focus on them as much as we needed them to cooperate with us, to take

the time to let our writers interview them, to allow me time to photograph them. Access, cooperation and time – they made my job easier, much easier. We had access and rudimentary equipment; today's photographers have sophisticated equipment unimagined in my day, and competition, lots and lots of competition. Burdens all around.

This collection of photos represents some of the many I took, mostly in the employ of *Rolling Stone*. Because these images will remain long after my departure from the music scene, I added some stories and facts to give the pictures context, to hint at what it was like to be with my cameras on the front lines of our changing world – a society characterized by the evolution of music and musicians and the infinite joy they gave us. To paraphrase Lou Gehrig, I was one of the very, very lucky guys.

Baron Wolman, May 2018.

JANN WENNER

1967 SAN FRANCISCO

(*above*) Jann Wenner, co-founder of *Rolling Stone*, in the magazine's original San Francisco offices.

BARON WOLMAN

1969 WOODSTOCK

(*left*) Photographer Baron Wolman at Woodstock with guitarist Carlos Santana in the background. Photo by the late great promoter, Bill Graham.

1967

Grateful Dead

1967 SAN FRANCISCO (RIGHT & OVERLEAF)

Would I survive my first *Rolling Stone* assignment? In 1967, I didn't yet personally know the Grateful Dead, they didn't know me, and *Rolling Stone* had not even published its first issue. Not to mention that the Dead were armed, locked and loaded, as far as I could tell. But Jann [Wenner] had told me to gather the members on the front steps of their 710 Ashbury Street house for a band portrait and I wasn't about to let him down. Easier said than done. I persisted, they obliged (more or less) and I lived to shoot (pictures) another day.

Grateful Dead

1967 SAN FRANCISCO

2017 was the fiftieth anniversary of *Rolling Stone* magazine. Who knew fifty years ago that this start-up publication would still be alive and well today? Immortalized and memorialized in issue no.1 is my very first assignment for the magazine. For that first issue we ran a feature story about the Grateful Dead pot bust. Our original editorial offices were down the alley from the San Francisco Hall of Justice. Directly across the street from that courthouse was where Jerry Barrish had opened his bail bond business, bailing out everybody from regular kids to famous movie and rock stars. And it was here, in October 1967, that I photographed members of the Dead posting bail for the bust. (Their lawyers, Brian Rohan and Michael Stepanian, are sitting in the convertible.)

B.B. King

1967 SAN FRANCISCO

For our 1967 photo session I met B.B. King at San Francisco's gorgeous Palace of the Legion of Honor. He was accompanied by his beloved guitar, Lucille. There had been, and there were to be, many other "Lucille's" but on this day B.B. brought along a gorgeous red instrument, probably a Gibson semi-hollow "ES" (Electric Spanish) model, the one he preferred at the time. I made a variety of informal portraits of King that day, one of which had him posed next to Rodin's "Thinker," a replica of which adorned the Court of Honor, and this one where the talented, beloved, and generous musician relaxed and looked into the lens of my Nikon… B.B. is sorely missed.

The Who

1967 SAN FRANCISCO

It was late 1967 and *Rolling Stone* had just produced their first issue. The Who were playing at the Cow Palace in San Francisco; they were opening for a band called The Association! The Who were something else, to say the least. Sporting the Edwardian look, Pete Townshend was at his best, performing his signature windmill move, smashing his guitar, then disappearing in a cloud of smoke while Keith Moon pounded his 'Pictures Of Lily' drum kit. Pete looked straight at me as if to say, "Welcome to the world of rock and roll."

The Who

In January 1968, *Rolling Stone* ran a story about The
Who which featured photos from my first live concert
assignment, a show at San Francisco's Cow Palace.
Jann Wenner was still writing for the magazine
and I was learning what it meant to be a rock and
roll photographer. It was at that concert that I first
encountered 'backstage', where it was and what was
happening there, and it was also at that concert that, to
my amazement and horror, I watched Pete Townshend
destroy his guitar. A guitarist demolishing his guitar
was akin to a photographer (me) hurling his Nikon
against the concrete floor, never to be used again. Or
so I thought, until a fresh guitar was brought out and
handed to Pete. As soon as the band left the stage I ran
up and grabbed the used smoke bomb, took it home
and photographed it as an objet d'art.

Johnny Cash

Scanning my archives recently, I came across this 1967 informal portrait of Johnny Cash, a photo I had long forgotten. The image had never been seen, never been published. I can't quite put my feelings into words but the picture speaks to me on some emotional, visceral level, and I find myself looking at it closely and often.

Johnny Cash

1967 SAN CARLOS

(*above*) This shot of Johnny Cash is one of the 'top of the list' images in my music archives. It was made on an early *Rolling Stone* assignment in December 1967, in Johnny's dressing room at the Circle Star Theatre a few minutes before he went onstage with his wife, June Carter Cash, who, if you look closely, is reflected in the mirror behind Johnny.

(*right*) Johnny Cash and June Carter Cash at the Circle Star Theatre, San Carlos, California (south of San Francisco), 1967. The Circle Star Theatre was a theatre in the round – the stage revolved and I had to wait for them to come around to get my best shots.

Haight Ashbury

1967 SAN FRANCISCO (LEFT & OVERLEAF)

(*left*) For years the Haight-Ashbury district of San Francisco, ground zero for the 1967 'Summer of Love', was a family residential neighborhood, one of the few spared from the devastating fires that followed the catastrophic earthquake of 1906. In the early sixties the counterculture people descended on the area and things changed dramatically. Families were displaced and older folks like this woman were confused by the arriving hordes of noisy, colorful young people. I was lucky to have lived in the Haight during the 'revolution', and to have documented the area's ever-changing landscape. Nothing is forever, of course. Today the Haight is much sought after by the newly tech-rich Millennials. Gentrification in the Haight has arrived and with it yet another upheaval is underway.

(*overleaf*) At the end of the Summer of Love, in a demo organized by the Diggers, residents of the Haight-Ashbury marched through the streets in early October 1967 (about the time the first issue of *Rolling Stone* was ready to roll off the presses), carrying a coffin to symbolize the 'Death of Hippie'. A funeral procession ended up in the Panhandle of Golden Gate Park. The protest was against the commercialization of the hippie movement. The Diggers maintained 'hippie' was a phenomenon created by the media. They may have been right.

Janet Planet

The media and Scott McKenzie exhorted 'Summer of Love' pilgrims to wear flowers in their hair. And many did, including my friend Janet Planet, the ex-wife of Van Morrison. (Today she is Janet Morrison Minto, a lovely woman who is fashioning equally lovely custom jewelry in Los Angeles.) For his part, McKenzie promised those who came to San Francisco that they would find a 'love-in', and in the streets there would be gentle people with flowers in their hair. There was certainly plenty of both to be seen, but the song's promise was mostly a fantasy, especially toward summertime's end. And with such high expectations came disappointments – homelessness, drug issues, poverty, to name a few. But then there were the flowers.

Ike & Tina Turner

1967 SAN FRANCISCO

Ike Turner, kickin' out the jams in the Ike & Tina Turner Revue in 1967, at the hungry-i in San Francisco's North Beach. According to Wikipedia, "Turner began playing piano and guitar when he was eight, forming his group, the Kings of Rhythm, as a teenager. He employed the group as his backing band for the rest of his life." Turner was born in Clarksdale, Mississippi, a recognized center for the genre known as the Delta Blues. He was married several times but, according to Tina, she was not one of his wives. In 1991, Ike & Tina Turner were inducted into the Rock and Roll Hall of Fame.

Ike & Tina Turner

1967 SAN FRANCISCO

In 1967, it was possible for a photographer to simply
walk up to the stage with his or her pro camera,
and – with consideration to the audience behind, of
course – take intimate up-close and personal photos of
well-known musicians, even those bound for greater
stardom. Here are Ike & Tina Turner performing
together in the Ike & Tina Turner Revue at the
popular hungry-i nightclub in San Francisco's North
Beach. In the late seventies, after the duo parted ways,
Tina started her soon-to-be-legendary solo career.

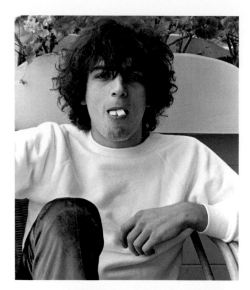

Pink Floyd

1967 SAUSALITO

I photographed Pink Floyd for *Rolling Stone* in 1967, in Sausalito, California, on the occasion of the band's initial, although ill-fated American tour. The first series of dates had to be cancelled when the band failed to get their work permits in time, and then again when their equipment failed to arrive on time. At the time I wrote: "Roger Waters [*bottom left*] is a British singer, songwriter, multi-instrumentalist, and composer. In 1965, he co-founded the progressive rock band, Pink Floyd. Syd Barrett [*top left*] is showing us one of his preferred ways to drop acid – using sugar cubes."

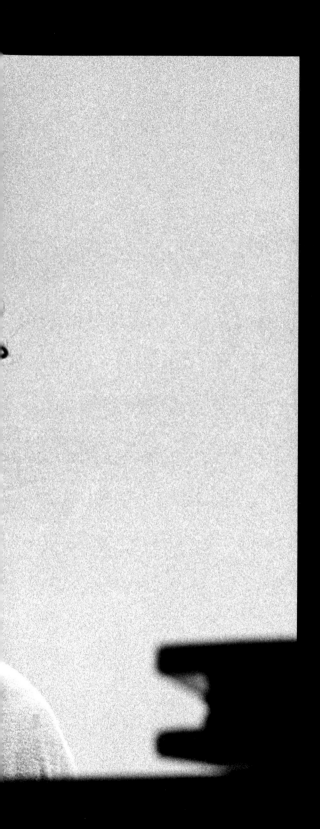

Little Richard

1967 SAN FRANCISCO

Up close and personal in 1967, with a rock and roll original, Little Richard. Think 'Tutti Frutti', 'Long Tall Sally' and 'Good Golly Miss Molly' if you want a quick dose of his hits. Born in Macon, Georgia in 1932, Little Richard's contributions to the world of popular music have been significant, his honors many. The Beatles opened for him in Hamburg, as did The Rolling Stones in the UK. Even Jimi Hendrix was a member of his band once upon a time.

Steve Miller

1967 SAN FRANCISCO (RIGHT & OVERLEAF)

(*right*) In 1967, I made this portrait of American guitarist and singer-songwriter Steve Miller for our then-new magazine *Rolling Stone* on the occasion of his signing with Capitol Records, with an advance of $50,000, a huge sum at the time. Nearly fifty years later, in 2017, he was inducted into the Rock and Roll Hall of Fame. His induction was well earned and fully justified. I've always enjoyed the company of Miller, from the day we made this photo in his San Francisco home at the edge of the Haight-Ashbury, to our various subsequent 'hangs'.

(*overleaf*) In 1967, in San Francisco's Golden Gate Park, I photographed what at the time was called The Steve Miller Blues Band for *Rolling Stone*. Miller had recently signed a contract with Capitol Records that was considered in quality and terms second only to The Beatles' Capitol agreement. From left to right, Boz Skaggs, Jim Peterman, Steve, Lonnie Turner, and Tim Davis. The band's first record for Capitol was *Children Of The Future*, released in '68. The album was produced by Glyn Johns and recorded in London's Olympic Studios. Olympic was as important a recording venue as the Abbey Road studios but due to copyright questions over the name Olympic, it was much less publicized. All the big name bands recorded at Olympic: the Stones, Jimi Hendrix, The Who, Led Zeppelin – the list goes on and it's a long one. The Steve Miller Band, as it became known, regularly changed band members and this picture was soon outdated.

Janis Joplin

1967 SAN FRANCISCO

Janis Joplin, on her bed at home in the Haight-Ashbury with her cat named Sam, San Francisco, 1967. Every time I photographed Janis I tried to tease out her award-winning smile. This is how I always remember Janis Joplin. She was one of my favorite subjects and I like to think my portraits of her reflect the affection I felt for her, that they allowed her singular brilliant light and indomitable spirit to come shining through.

Janis Joplin

1967 SAN FRANCISCO
(LEFT & PREVIOUS PAGE)

My kind of rock concert. Small, intimate, 'all access'
for everyone to everything (including the stage) and
everybody (including the band). Look how the kids are
hanging out at the edge of the stage – can you imagine
that happening today? In 1967, I photographed Big
Brother & The Holding Company with Janis Joplin
here at McNears Beach Park in Marin County,
California, a few miles north across the Golden Gate
Bridge from San Francisco. This is the way it was in
the early days of *Rolling Stone*, warm and friendly free
gatherings, with music for the people. Big Brother
& The Holding Company was a San Francisco band
formed in 1965 by the well-known local promoter,
Chet Helms. Wikipedia writes, "Their 1968 album,
Cheap Thrills, is considered one of the masterpieces of
the psychedelic sound of San Francisco." The version
of the band seen here included Peter Albin (bass and
guitar), Dave Getz (drums and piano), Sam Andrew
(guitar and vocals), James Gurley (guitar and bass), and,
of course, Janis doing the lead vocals.

Jim Morrison

1967 SAN FRANCISCO

Although it may appear otherwise, I photographed
most musicians only once or twice during the relatively
short time my cameras were focused mainly on music.
So it was with Jim Morrison and The Doors; one time
only, in December 1967, at Bill Graham's Winterland
Auditorium in San Francisco. While I enjoyed all-
access all the time, I decided to photograph The Doors
from the point of view of the audience. I pushed my
way forward through the crowd to the front of the stage
and suffered thirty minutes of severe claustrophobia,
hardly able to change lenses in that sardine-can-like
environment. I shot only two rolls at this concert…
two rolls standing among the crowd, in the front row,
pushed against the barrier, little me, like tiny fish
packed tightly in a can. Never again. Difficult to see
in detail, in the contact sheet here is Jim Morrison
caressing, embracing, and stroking the microphone as
only he could. I am particularly fond of the shot of Jim
smiling. How seldom did we see a Jim Morrison smile,
which is understandable now knowing of his tortured
soul. "There are things known and things unknown,
and in between are the doors of perception." *Aldous
Huxley*

Procol Harum

1967 SAN FRANCISCO

Procol Harum was a British rock band formed in mid-1967, shortly before I took this photo in November in San Francisco. They arrived at the same time as Pink Floyd with whom they shared the bill at Bill Graham's Fillmore West. A week later they appeared with The Doors at the same venue. Procol Harum started touring in support of their massive hit, 'A Whiter Shade of Pale'. In fact, their live debut was opening for Jimi Hendrix! The band was named after their manager's Burmese cat: "... her face turned a whiter shade of pale."

Phil Spector

1967 OAKLAND

On the very day that Jann Wenner asked me if I wanted to be the photographer for a yet unnamed music publication, Phil Spector was happily praying to some unidentified gods for some undisclosed supplications. Spector had his Wall of Sound, I had my Tri-X. Spector had his guns and girlfriends, I had my Nikons. Beyond all of that, all I know is that on this April day in 1967, at Mills College in Oakland, California, my life changed in extraordinary and unanticipated ways. Spector eventually went to jail. I eventually became *Rolling Stone*'s first chief photographer. Our futures were both set in stone.

1968

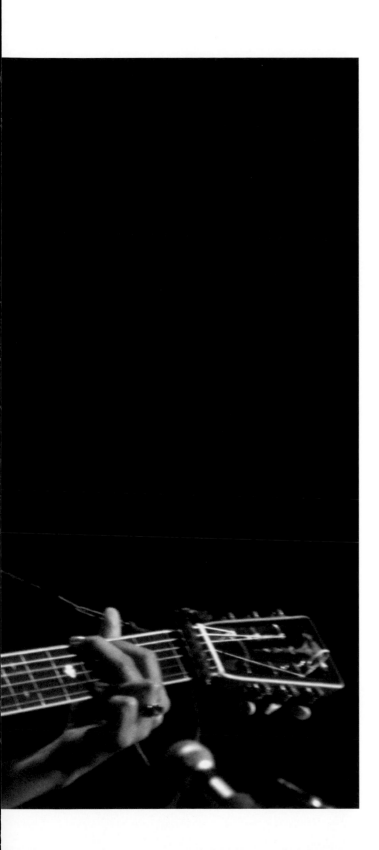

Joan Baez

1968 MADISON

Respect for the musician. The
beginning of the end for music
photographers? Many years ago
I photographed the lovely Joan
Baez in concert – as usual she sang
and played her acoustic guitar.
As the concert began I heard the
unmistakable clacking of the
mirror from numerous single lens
reflex film cameras. Joan heard
them, too. She stopped singing
and said something to the effect,
"I'm flattered that you want to
photograph me, but your cameras
are quite noisy and folks are here
for the music. Tell you what – for
two songs feel free to take all the
pictures you want. But after those
two songs, please put your cameras
down and enjoy the music."
I think that may have begun what
is now the standard for concert
music photographers everywhere:
two songs and then go home...
In one sense, understandable.
In another, regrettable.

Jimi Hendrix

1968 SAN FRANCISCO

There was such elegance about Jimi Hendrix. At rest
and even during his 'creative wild moments' on stage
he radiated a sense of integrity. I continue to say it was
impossible to take a bad picture of Jimi, a statement not
about my photographic skills, rather speaking about
the man, the persona, the pensive shooting star who
all too briefly graced us with his music, his inspired
lyrics, and, yes, his spiritual presence. Earlier in the day
between the first and second of his four San Francisco
concerts at Bill Graham's Fillmore Auditorium in
February 1968, we met Jimi at his motel on Fisherman's
Wharf. As the writer was interviewing a surprisingly
sedate Hendrix, I was shooting informal, natural light
portraits, one of which was used on the issue no. 26
cover of *Rolling Stone* …

Jimi Hendrix

1968 SAN FRANCISCO (RIGHT & OVERLEAF)

I often say I 'saw' the music; I was always looking for those visual magical musical moments that caught the essence of a live action performance in a static image. With film cameras we had thirty-five frames per roll, thirty-five chances to make a really good photograph. If I got two or three outstanding pictures per roll I considered the shoot successful. When I look at the contact sheets from the two Jimi Hendrix Experience concerts I shot in 1968 in San Francisco, I see more than twenty amazing photos on each roll! Something magical was happening on those nights. I was so completely in sync with the trio, it felt somehow as if I were actually a member of the band. They were playing their Fenders and Gibsons, and I was playing my Nikons. On stage Jimi met my test of musical and performing excellence; he was the consummate entertainer whether he was pointing at me or lost in the ecstasy of a rock and roll concert that produced an image I call my 'money shot'.

Lacy

1968 SAN FRANCISCO

Lacy's eyes... and feathers, San
Francisco, 1968. "Nobody doesn't
love a groupie!"

Lacy

1968 SAN FRANCISCO

In November of 1968, from the moment she walked into my studio I couldn't take my eyes off Lacy. She was sultry, sensuous and downright gorgeous… and definitely stoned. I loved photographing her; she fell into poses so naturally. I spread copies of *Rolling Stone* in front of her and put a joint in her hand – why, I don't remember, it seemed like the right thing to do at the time. In the end, one of those photos graced *Rolling Stone*'s first and only holiday card sent to subscribers. Presumably, Lacy is still in the San Francisco Bay Area but we can't seem to find her, although her photo day in the studio lives on in my memory… as it would yours.

Mick Jagger

1968 LONDON

OK, I want what he's got! The long hair. The smile. The lips. The silk shirt. The elegant matching vest. The Polaroid Land 101 Automatic Camera. His voice. His band. His talent. The women. His seemingly endless career. In short, I want his life. In 1968, I was on the set of the film *Performance* in London where I made this shot of a smiling 25-year-old Michael Philip Jagger. I was 31. The film, produced in 1968 but not released until 1970, opened to mixed reviews. Those reviews notwithstanding, I personally liked what I saw here.

Nicky Hopkins

1968 SAN FRANCISCO

Nicky Hopkins, hugely talented British keyboard player. Due to his frail health, Hopkins was mostly a session musician, recording with some of the world's great bands, including The Who, Kinks, Rolling Stones, and John and George post-Beatle. I photographed him here in San Francisco in 1968, when he was on a short tour with the Jeff Beck Group. He appears with the band on their memorable albums, *Truth* and *Beck-Ola*.

Fats Domino

1968 LAS VEGAS

The American pianist and singer-songwriter Fats
Domino was in Las Vegas preparing for his evening
appearance as a lounge musician (the best lounge act
ever!) when I photographed him here. It was a privilege
to be allowed into his dressing room with my cameras.
Check out the bling and the red velvet pants. Fats was
born in New Orleans in 1928, into a musical family.
Five of his records released before 1955 sold over a
million copies and were certified gold. He was awarded
the Grammy Lifetime Achievement Award in 1987.
By the end of his career, Domino had sold more records
than any other fifties rocker except Elvis Presley! His
1956 interpretation of 'Blueberry Hill' was his biggest
hit, one that sticks in my mind even today.

Mike Bloomfield

1968 SAN FRANCISCO

On the left, Mike Bloomfield, another extraordinarily brilliant guitarist who left us much too early. On the right a pensive Mike Bloomfield, at his home in Mill Valley, California, in 1968, during a long conversation with Jann Wenner for the *Rolling Stone* Interview. Bloomfield was a hugely talented American musician, much loved for his astounding guitar playing, and very influential in the revival of classic blues music. He died in 1981, at age 37, another career cut short by drugs.

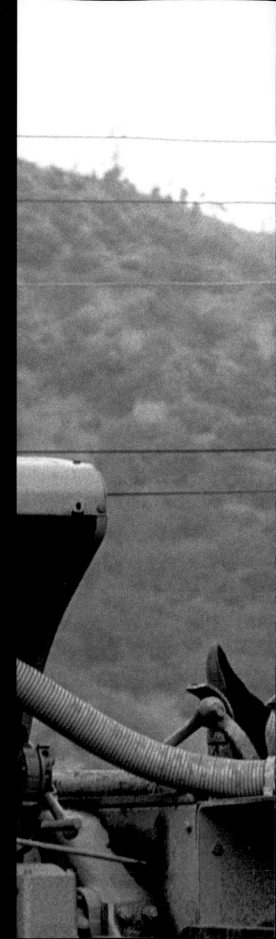

Frank Zappa

1968 LOS ANGELES

Frank Zappa in a cave behind his house atop Laurel
Canyon in Los Angeles, 1968, posing for a major
Rolling Stone story. This shot made the cover of issue
no. 14. One never knew what the talented and eccentric Frank Zappa would serve up next. On the right he
tries to drive the ancient D7 bulldozer rusting behind
his rented log cabin house – which once belonged to
silent film star Tom Mix – high above Laurel Canyon
Boulevard in Los Angeles.

Frank Zappa

1968 LOS ANGELES

In May, 1968, writer Jerry Hopkins and I visited Frank at his home at the top of Laurel Canyon in Los Angeles to write and photograph the cover story for *Rolling Stone* issue no. 14. Among the many visual delights Frank offered up that day was a personal demonstration of the rope swing he had installed for his kids well, not really, as only Moon had been born by then so maybe the swing was actually his? Above, the ever-articulate Zappa issues a hypothetical pronouncement, "WTF is going on over there in DC, Donald? You don't get it, do you? Must I, Citizen Frank Zappa, return to Earth to give you a lesson in civics? The Constitution of the United States of America starts with the words 'We the People', NOT 'I the President!' C'mon, man, get with the program."

Booker T. & The M.G.'s

1968 SAN FRANCISCO

Where else to photograph Booker T. & The M.G.'s than in a red MG? In this 1968 photo I shot the band behind the wheel of its namesake. Left to right: Duck Dunn (bass guitar), Al Jackson, Jr. (drums), Steve Cropper (guitar), and Booker T. Jones (organ and piano). This instrumental R&B/funk band was influential in shaping the sounds of Southern and Memphis soul, and was the house band of Stax Records. According to *The Encyclopedia of Popular Music*: "Their intuitive interplay became the bedrock of Stax Records, the foundation on which the label and the studio was built. The quartet appeared on all the company's notable releases." The band was inducted into the Rock and Roll Hall of Fame in 1992.

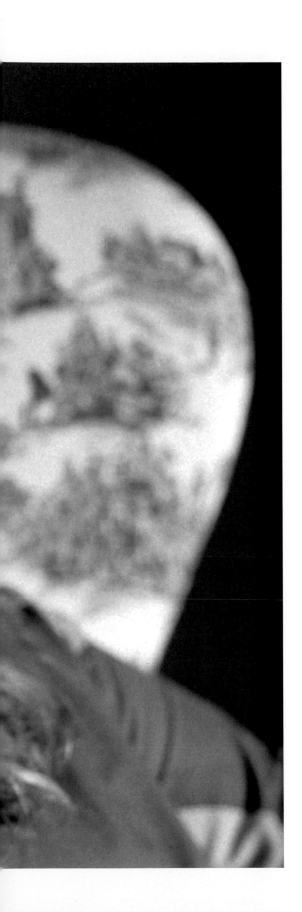

Mama Cass

1968 LOS ANGELES

Mama Cass Elliot (born Ellen Naomi Cohen) of The
Mamas & The Papas, Los Angeles, relaxed during a
1968 interview for *Rolling Stone* in Los Angeles. Cass
passed away in her sleep in 1974 at age 32, following
a concert in London. After The Mamas & The Papas
broke up in 1969, Cass released five solo albums and
even headlined at Caesar's Palace in Las Vegas. In 1998,
the entire band was inducted into the Rock and Roll
Hall of Fame.

Smokey Robinson

1968 SAN FRANCISCO

Smokey Robinson singing the Motown hit, 'The Tracks of My Tears', San Francisco, 1968. I made these photos of Smokey fifty years ago at Bimbo's 365 Club, a San Francisco tradition since 1931, and still going strong, as is Smokey, the founder and front man of the Motown vocal group, The Miracles. Robinson was inducted into the Rock and Roll Hall of Fame in 1987, and was also awarded the Library of Congress Gershwin Prize for his lifetime contribution to popular music.

Sun Ra

1968 BERKELEY

Sun Ra, Berkeley, California, 1968. One of the most extraordinary characters in twentieth-century jazz, Sun Ra (born Herman Sonny Blount) claimed to have arrived on Earth from the planet Saturn. "Some call me Mr Ra, some call me Mr Re. You can call me Mr Mystery," he told countless audiences. Leading his 'Arkestra' for over thirty years, his performances included dancers in futuristic costumes and innovative electronic instruments that were widely used in jazz. Wikipedia writes, "He made his mark in a wider cultural context, proclaiming African origins of jazz, and affirming black pride and spirituality in his music." He left planet Earth in 1993.

Janis Joplin

1968 SAN FRANCISCO

This photo of Janis Joplin is one of my favorites. I made her portrait in 1968, in the colorful loft of my good friend Spaulding Taylor. I was on assignment for *EYE* magazine, the oversized glossy *Rolling Stone* 'wannabe' published briefly – only fifteen issues – by the Hearst corporation. (There are copies for sale on eBay.) Janis was in a good mood that day – just look at that smile and the elegant way she holds herself. Royalty! Since I always saw her as one of the queens of rock and roll, why not pose her in a throne? So I did.

Janis Joplin

1968 SAN FRANCISCO

(*left*) Janis Joplin in my Haight-Ashbury studio, 1968.
For an assignment I needed a quick color photo of
Janis in performance but she had nothing scheduled
so I convinced her to bring a microphone to the shoot
along with a tape of her most recent album so she could
lip-synch during our faux concert. I simulated stage
lighting and, yes, she lip-synched briefly but couldn't
hold back her innate desire to sing and proceeded
to gift me one hour of full tilt Joplin boogie! An
experience I always lovingly refer to as my 'concert
for one'.

Big Brother & The Holding Company

1968 SAN FRANCISCO (OVERLEAF)

Big Brother & The Holding Company at the Palace of
Fine Arts in San Francisco, 1968. One of my favorite
shots of the band, the photo includes (left to right):
Dave Getz, Peter Albin, Janis Joplin, James Gurley and
Sam Andrew.

The Who

1968 LONDON

(*above*) Although The Who's energetic (to put it mildly) drummer Keith Moon passed away pretty much ten years to the day after I made this photo in London in 1968, I've always imagined the picture reflected a premonition of his early demise. Not that he didn't help the process along – his behavior was widely understood as 'irregular' and often self-destructive. Or was he thinking here of some song lyrics he had written exhorting an anonymous listener to please talk to him again?

(*right*) John Entwistle, bass guitarist for The Who, in the studio recording the rock opera, *Tommy*, London, 1968. Entwistle was the only member of the band to have had any formal music training.

(*overleaf*) It was thrilling, almost mesmerizing, as I watched and photographed The Who record their iconic rock opera *Tommy*. The band started recording the album in September 1968, at London's IBC Studios. I appeared with my cameras for *Rolling Stone* shortly thereafter. In the beginning there was actually no firm title for the album but Townshend eventually settled on *Tommy* because it was simply a common British name, as well as a nickname for soldiers in World War I. Here are Pete and bassist John Entwistle collaborating, on something – what I don't recall. I just really like this shot.

The Who

1968 LONDON

The Who recording the rock opera *Tommy* in London, 1968. John Entwistle, Roger Daltrey, Pete Townshend and Kit Lambert. Keith Moon was in the other room. I'm still fascinated by their sartorial choices for a day's work in the studio: Entwistle in a formal suit, Daltrey sporting his fringe top, Townshend in a simple T-sh

Grace Slick

1968 SAN FRANCISCO

(*above*) Shoot me if you must, but shoot me with a rose! Grace Slick in my Haight-Ashbury studio in 1968. Slick was an American singer, songwriter, and model, now a well-known artist. When I first knew her she was the lead singer of Jefferson Airplane, another San Francisco homegrown band. My faves: 'White Rabbit', and 'Somebody To Love' with the Airplane, and 'We Built This City' with her later band Starship. The city they claimed to have built was San Francisco, and build it they did...

(*right*) Grace Slick was 29 when I photographed her in San Francisco in 1968 for *EYE* magazine. With seductively liquid lips and wearing her signature Girl Scout uniform, she was the picture of innocence. Hmmm... I'm flattered that Slick, currently an applauded artist, painted her version of this photo to use as her signature 'brand' image.

Grace Slick

1968 SAN FRANCISCO

(*left*) Grace Slick of Jefferson Airplane with pasta, San Francisco, 1968. Grace always brought something unique to the table. Pun intended ...

(*above*) Grace Slick is widely known for her role in the sixties' San Francisco psychedelic music scene. Her career spanned four decades, most notably with the bands Jefferson Airplane, Jefferson Starship, and Starship. Two decades later she became (at age 47) the oldest female vocalist to reach the number one position on the US Billboard's Hot 100, this time with Starship's 'We Built This City'. I always delighted in shooting delightfully eccentric Grace and fell in love through my lens every time I photographed her... like this 1968 informal portrait session in my Haight-Ashbury studio. These days Grace is a widely exhibited portrait painter who considers her visual artistry another extension of the artistic temperament that landed her in the music scene in the first place.

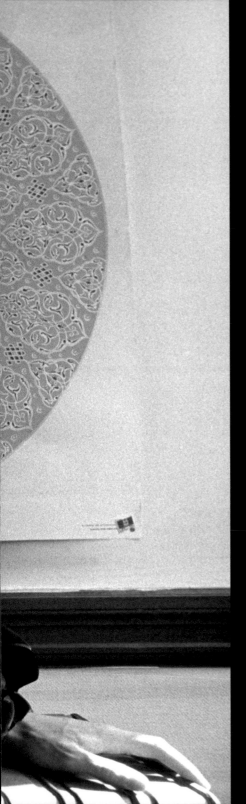

Jack Casady

1968 SAN FRANCISCO

Bassist Jack Casady, pictured here in 1968, in a custom shirt made by then-tailor, Jeanne Colon. At the time, Casady was a member of Jefferson Airplane, one of the San Francisco-based bands that pioneered psychedelic rock. Today, Casady plays with Hot Tuna, an American blues band formed in 1969 by him and guitarist Jorma Kaukonen. The band began playing during a break in the Airplane's touring schedule when Grace Slick underwent minor vocal cord surgery that left her temporarily unable to sing. As Hot Tuna, Casady, Kaukonen, Paul Kantner and drummer Joey Covington played several shows around the San Francisco Bay Area. When the Airplane resumed touring, Hot Tuna actually became one of their opening acts. Although other musicians have come and gone during the group's many incarnations, the name Hot Tuna has become shorthand for Jack Casady and Jorma Kaukonen. Hot Tuna is still active and still touring after all these years. Meanwhile, Jeanne Colon changed her name and her profession. No longer making clothes for rock bands, she is now Jeanne Rose, a highly trained, highly respected herbalist who has written more than twenty books on the subject, lectures extensively and teaches herbs, aromatherapy and distillation techniques around the world.

Rod Stewart

1968 SAN FRANCISCO

It's been nearly five decades since I photographed Rod
Stewart in 1968, performing with the great Jeff Beck
Group in San Francisco. In the current (no. 1245)
issue of *Rolling Stone*, led in with a fabulous portrait
by photographer Peggy Sirota, Stewart is described
as "a natural-born crowd-pleaser for whom life has
been very good for a very long time". He's twice been
inducted into the Rock and Roll Hall of Fame, first for
his own contribution to the genre, second as a member
of the Faces. Me, I'm partial to his 1971 solo album,
Every Picture Tells A Story, fully believing the truth of
these words.

Howlin' Wolf

1968 SAN FRANCISCO

It was Howlin'Wolf who wrote 'Smokestack Lightning', one of his most popular and influential songs. Hey, when you're blue, you're blue, nothin' much to do about it but sing. Chester Arthur Burnett, known as Howlin'Wolf, was a Chicago blues singer, guitarist and harmonica player. There is something I quite like about this 1968 portrait I made of him – for me, musicians don't always have to be playing for their own unique and distinct humanity to be evident. Originally from Mississippi, with his booming voice and looming physical presence (6'3", 275 pounds), he was one of the best-known Chicago blues artists. In 1952, when Chess Records secured his contract, Howlin'Wolf relocated from Arkansas to Chicago where he formed a new band, recruiting Jody Williams from Memphis Slim's band as his first guitarist. Within a year he'd enticed legendary guitarist Hubert Sumlin to leave Memphis and join him in Chicago; Sumlin's understated solos perfectly complemented Burnett's huge voice. In the early sixties, Howlin' Wolf recorded several famous songs, including 'Wang Dang Doodle', 'Back Door Man', 'The Red Rooster' (later known as 'The Little Red Rooster'), and others. Several became part of the repertoires of British and American rock groups who further popularized them. In the end, Wolf was so financially successful – a rarity among blues musicians – that he was able to offer band members not only a decent salary, but benefits such as health insurance; this in turn enabled him to hire his pick of available musicians and keep his band one of the best. Howlin'Wolf passed away in 1976; on his gravestone are etched both a guitar and a harmonica.

Richie Havens

1968 SAN FRANCISCO

Richie Havens captured here on stage in San Francisco.
With his unmistakably intense musical style, Havens
opened the weekend of Peace, Love and Music with
a three-hour performance at Woodstock which, like
Santana's, was a game changer for his career. His
improvisation of the spiritual 'Motherless Child'
morphed into 'Freedom', which became one of his
signature songs. An American singer-songwriter and
guitarist, Havens' father was a Blackfoot Indian, his
mother from the West Indies. At age 20, he moved
to New York's Greenwich Village where his popular
solo performances led to a contract with legendary
manager Albert Grossman. Havens later added acting
to his repertoire and became an environmental activist.
After his death in 2013, as per his wishes, Havens' ashes
were scattered by plane over the site of the original
Woodstock festival.

The GTOs

1968 LOS ANGELES

(*above*) Everyone loves a groupie! I first photographed Miss Mercy (Peters) before I knew who she was. In 1967, she was sitting in Golden Gate Park with two friends. Heavily mascaraed, she immediately caught my eye. I asked if I could take their picture, pointed my Nikon at them and voilà, instant immortality! That's what photography can do for a person since the picture I took that day ended up on page 1 of *Rolling Stone* issue no. 6. Who knew that only a year later I would encounter and photograph Mercy again as a member of the famous GTOs.

(*right*) The GTOs were a 'groupie group' consisting of young women from LA, most of whom were regulars on the Sunset Strip scene in the late sixties. In 1969, they released their only record, *Permanent Damage*. Frank Zappa took them under his wing, producing their album and generally raising their profile. There has always been some confusion as to what GTO stands for: writer Stanley Booth suggested Girls Together Outrageously, which was used on their album, but other suggestions include Girls Together Occasionally, Often and Only.

Pamela Des Barres

1968 LOS ANGELES

In November 1968 in Los Angeles, I took this photograph of a coquettish Pamela des Barres, aka 'Miss Pamela' and born Pamela Ann Miller, justifiably known these days as the 'Queen of the Groupies'. To her might be attributed the entire genre of 'groupie', although throughout history women who love music have also loved those who produce it. However, Pamela may have been the first young woman who openly and publicly had a plan to meet the musicians and celebrities about whom she dreamed. Furthermore, she brought a definite joie de vivre to the sixties music scene, an obvious enjoyment of life that still delights us today. Her early books, *I'm With The Band* and *Take Another Little Piece of My Heart: A Groupie Grows Up*, are both entertaining and enlightening reads. Her latest book, *Let It Bleed: How to Write a Rockin' Memoir*, guides women through the process of writing their memoirs, and her assignments in Femoir have

Lou Adler

1968 LOS ANGELES

If you aren't familiar with Lou Adler, well, you should be. Among his many talents he is a record producer and film director (also an inductee into the Rock and Roll Hall of Fame). In 1967, he produced the legendary Monterey Pop Festival and the subsequent film, *Monterey Pop*. He produced The Mamas & The Papas and Carole King, to name but a few. He won a Grammy for King's album, *Tapestry*. Eight years after I shot this photo of Adler in his home in 1968, he was kidnapped and then released after a $25K ransom payment! He currently owns the well-known Roxy Theater nightclub on the Sunset Strip in West Hollywood, itself overflowing with rock and roll history.

Joni Mitchell

1968 LOS ANGELES

Joni Mitchell at home in Laurel Canyon, in Los
Angeles, 1968. The song 'Our House' was written by
Graham Nash while he was living with Joni (and her
two cats) in this very house where I made the picture.
After the photo session we sat around drinking tea,
talking about life and love, heartbreak and passion, and
wars that do not end…

B.B. King

1968 SAN FRANCISCO

The ecstasy of performance. The joy of music. B.B. King in 1968 – out of focus, nothing sharp… except his, and our, infinite elation. It's why we loved him, why we go to concerts, why music moves us unconditionally.

Jeff Beck

1968 LOS ANGELES & SAN FRANCISCO (BELOW & OVERLEAF)

(*left*) Jeff Beck is always practicing! Here he runs through licks in his room at the Chateau Marmont on Sunset Boulevard in Los Angeles.

(*below*) On tour with the Jeff Beck Group, 1968. There is something about this image and its components that always draws my eyes to it for more than a moment.

(*overleaf*) In 1968, when guitar legend and dedicated car nut Jeff Beck asked me if I knew where he might buy an American hot rod, I said I did and took him to the auto dealer who had one in his San Francisco showroom. Beck liked what he saw and put his money on the table for this stylish custom machine. Unfortunately, the hot rod never made it across the pond to Jeff's car collection. I recall asking him why – some complicated technical import issues, I think. Recent rumors have it that Beck is hoping to locate the car and finally bring it 'home'.

Taj Mahal

1968 TOPANGA CANYON

Taj Mahal (born Henry Saint Clair Fredericks, Jr., by the way) is an American blues musician. I didn't realize that he was self-taught but nevertheless plays several instruments, probably due to the fact that his father was also a musician. His stage name came to him in a dream about Gandhi and India. I photographed him here in 1968, at his then-home in Topanga Canyon near Los Angeles. Taj was raised in a musical environment; his mother was a member of a local gospel choir and his father was an Afro-Caribbean jazz arranger and piano player. Taj has done much to reshape the definition and scope of blues music over the course of his almost fifty-year career, fusing it with nontraditional forms, including sounds from the Caribbean, Africa and the South Pacific.

→ 22   → 22A   → 23   → 23A

→ 28   → 28A   → 29   → 29A

KODAK SAFETY FILM

→ 24   G   J   L

S'AFETY   FILM

→ 30   → 30 A

Van Dyke Parks

1968 LOS ANGELES

Van Dyke Parks is an American composer, arranger, record producer, instrumentalist, singer-songwriter, author and actor. He has collaborated with the best, from Brian Wilson and The Beach Boys to The Byrds to Randy Newman to Harry Nilsson to Ringo Starr and more – it's a long, long list. Plus he has released several successful studio albums of his own recordings. As an actor he played Little Tommy Manicotti on Jackie Gleason's *The Honeymooners*, and even performed onstage with Frank Zappa's Mothers of Invention. These shots of Van Dyke were taken long ago, in 1968, at his home in Los Angeles.

Steve Winwood

1968 SAN FRANCISCO

(*above*) In early 1968, the talented British multi-instrumentalist Steve Winwood became our first celebrity guest at *Rolling Stone*'s recently opened offices in San Francisco. Primarily a vocalist and keyboard player, the musical genres of multi-faceted Winwood include rock, blue-eyed soul, rhythm and blues, blues rock, pop rock and jazz. Playing with the band Traffic when he visited us, he was also a significant member of The Spencer Davis Group and Blind Faith, and more recently has led his own groups under his own name. Winwood was inducted into the Rock and Roll Hall of Fame as a member of Traffic in 2004. Here in 1968, he looked so young, so innocent.

(*right*) Fifty years ago, directly adjacent to and on the same floor as the first *Rolling Stone* offices in San Francisco, sat the mammoth Linotype machines. Linotype was a hot metal typesetting system that cast blocks of metal type for setting small-size body text for newspapers, magazines, etc., from the late nineteenth century until the 1970s. The name of the machine comes from the fact that it produces an entire line of metal type at once, hence 'line-o'-type'. Here in early 1968, Winwood examines a 'line of type', words which would soon find their way into the pages of the new publication.

Eric Burdon

1968 LOS ANGELES

Another blast from the past! Here is Eric Burdon, the British singer-songwriter, in his Los Angeles home in 1968. Burdon is best known as a member of The Animals and the funk band, War. As a total aside, I learned from various media reports that, in 1967, Burdon married Angela King, whom he 'stole' from Animals guitarist Andy Summers, and who Eric describes in his autobiography as "a beautiful Anglo-Indian woman with absolutely perfect breasts". The next year she left him for, among others, Jimi Hendrix; she and Burdon were subsequently divorced. She was murdered in 1996 by yet another estranged boyfriend. Ah, the vicissitudes of rock and roll love.

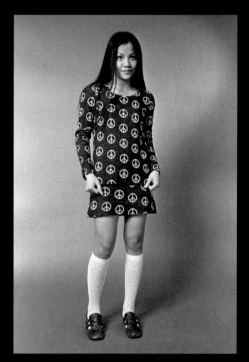

1969

Clarence Carter

1969 MACON, GEORGIA

In 1969, I was in Macon, Georgia, with the *Rolling Stone* writer; we were working on a piece about the music of Macon and Muscle Shoals (Alabama) which unfortunately was never published. Nevertheless, I returned home with some outstanding musician photos, of which this portrait of Clarence Carter is one. Clarence was born blind but obtained a good education in spite of his handicap, graduating with a Bachelor of Science degree in music. Carter is an American blues and soul singer, songwriter and record producer. The song of his that I remember best is 'Slip Away': "Without him knowin' you're gone, Baby we could meet somewhere, Somewhere we both are not known. Can you slip away, slip away?" Writer Brian Ward declared that Carter "virtually made a career from tales of unbridled love and illicit sex..." At age 80, Clarence Carter continues to write, continues to record and continues to tour.

Joni Mitchell

1969 NEWPORT, RHODE ISLAND

Joni Mitchell is a Canadian singer-songwriter whom *Rolling Stone* described as: "one of the greatest songwriters ever." I photographed her at the Newport Folk Festival, Rhode Island, in 1969. More recently, in 2015, it was confirmed that Mitchell had suffered a brain aneurysm and that while speech was difficult, she had been communicating with others. By July 2015, Mitchell was back at home, undergoing physical therapy and 'making progress', according to her lawyer. In October 2015, Mitchell's friend, singer Judy Collins, reported that Joni was taking part in rehabilitation every day and was walking, talking and painting. Mitchell made her first public appearance following the aneurysm when she attended a Chick Corea concert in Los Angeles in August 2016.

Grateful Dead

1969 SAN FRANCISCO

It wasn't until 1969 that *Rolling Stone* finally did a cover story on the Grateful Dead. For issue no. 40, and one of the few times I photographed a band in my photo studio, I decided to shoot the Dead in the style of two of my photographic heroes, Irving Penn and Richard Avedon, very simply against a 'studio gray' background with a single light in order to make simple yet incisive individual portraits of the band members. On the far left is Bob Weir who played rhythm guitar and sang many of the lead vocals through all of the Dead's thirty-year career. On the center left is Bill Kreutzmann, the Dead's drummer, relaxing on a rocker in the studio for the shoot. (This photo featured on the cover of Kreutzmann's autobiography, *Deal*.) On the center right is Mickey Hart, the band's Grammy award-winning percussionist. On the far right is Jerry Garcia, nominally the leader of the band, publicly showing the world for the first time his missing digit, the piece of his finger accidentally chopped off by his brother when they were very young.

Little Richard

1969 SAN FRANCISCO

It's only rock and roll but we love it, don't we! And so do
I and so does Little Richard – obviously – here in my
1969 shot of him live at the Fillmore in San Francisco.
His dynamic music and charismatic showmanship
laid the foundation for rock and roll. Little Richard's
onstage antics – running on and off the stage, lifting his
leg while playing the piano, and jumping up and down
atop the piano – brought audiences into a frenzy. Yep,
rock and roll sure can do that to ya. Did then, does now.

Country Joe & The Fish

1969 SAN QUENTIN PRISON

San Quentin Prison, California, 1969. Country Joe &
The Fish performed a free concert for prison inmates
under the auspices of Bread and Roses ('Hope and
Healing Through Live Music'), the non-profit founded
by Mimi Farina, Joan Baez's younger sister. In what to
me was thoughtless planning akin to waterboarding,
the band brought along a couple of young women
in mini-dresses who danced seductively in front of a
crowd of men who, of course, were strictly forbidden
from coming near the women, let alone having any
bodily contact with them. Good music accompanied
by an insensitive gesture that could have easily caused
a riot. Yes, I was nervous, happy when we left and the
gates closed behind us.

Donovan

Donovan ('Mellow Yellow'), in Los Angeles, 1969, when I was assigned to shoot him for *Vogue*, believe it or not. Donovan (Leitch) is a Scottish singer, songwriter and guitarist. He first became popular thanks to his live performances on the UK TV series, *Ready Steady Go!* His many hit singles included 'Sunshine Superman' and 'Mellow Yellow', the latter rumored to be about getting high by smoking dried banana skins. Donovan later admitted the lyric phrase 'electrical banana' referred to a vibrator. He was inducted into the Rock and Roll Hall of Fame in 2012.

Mick Jagger

1969 OAKLAND

These were taken in November 1969, the very first time I photographed The Rolling Stones. It was also the band's first US tour since July 1966, after a hiatus due to drug charges and the complications therefrom. It was also Mick Taylor's first tour with the band; he had recently replaced Brian Jones. Although rock critic Robert Christgau called it 'history's first mythic rock and roll tour', it ended darkly in December with the Altamont free concert. Terry Reid, B.B. King (replaced on some dates by Chuck Berry), and Ike & Tina Turner were the supporting acts; Janis Joplin even joined Ike & Tina at one of the Madison Square Garden concerts. I've always liked how Keith Richards appears in the lower left of this shot, with Mick Jagger in center stage, a role that seemed often to be repeated. It was also on this tour that Sam Cutler, the tour's road manager, began introducing the Stones as "the greatest rock and roll band in the world". And I guess it could be argued they pretty much still are.

Mick Jagger

1969 NEW YORK

At a New York City press conference (in the Rainbow Room), and on the cover of *Rolling Stone* issue no. 49 in November of 1969, Mick Jagger promised San Francisco a free Stones concert. Altamont Raceway got the concert, not Golden Gate Park as planned. The result was a well-attended gathering at a dirt track in the hills east of the City, a concert that might have been 'Woodstock West' but in the end is remembered for the violence that occurred on that cold, damp day.

the
Bottom Shelf
The Friends Bookstore

124 S. Mission
Fallbrook, CA
(760) 451-9606
bottomshelfbookstore.org

Operated by
Friends of the Fallbrook Library

All proceeds benefit the library

Woodstock

1969 WOODSTOCK

No one could have predicted the enduring influence of the Woodstock experience. Yes, the bands were first-rate and there were many of them. And the location, isolated in nature as it was, was picture-perfect and tranquil, a bucolic setting for relaxing with friends and listening to music and getting high. But in unexpected ways, Woodstock became more than an oversize music concert. I was fascinated, captivated, enchanted and transfixed by the crowd, the hundreds of thousands of kind and gentle souls who made the trek to Yasgur's farm. It was the people upon whom I focused my cameras. I wandered among them daily, taking pictures, building a personal diary of three miraculous days that I somehow knew were both a promise and an aberration. We held out hope that the former would characterize our future lives. Yet, as we look back, we realize with great sadness it was the latter that became the world we live in today.

Iggy Pop

1969 MOUNT CLEMENS

I was shooting the Ann Arbor Blues Festival in August, 1969, when I heard talk about another musical event sixty-five miles northeast of Ann Arbor called the Mount Clemens Pop Festival. The line-up was impressive with, among others: Eric Burdon, John Mayall, MC5, Alice Cooper and Iggy & The Stooges, the one band I photographed and then only briefly because I arrived so late. Man, how I yearn for the days when we music photographers could walk right up to the stage with our cameras – actually get on the stage with the bands – and make the kind of memorable photos only possible with up-close and personal access. Oh, well, that was then and this is now. This was the first and only time I saw or photographed Iggy & The Stooges.

Miles Davis

1969 NEW YORK

In 1969, after I made some (soulful) black & white informal portraits of Miles Davis in his New York City West Side brownstone, we headed out in his beloved Ferrari 275GTB onto the West Side Highway toward legendary Gleason's Gym in the Bronx for his every-other-day workout in the boxing ring. Along the way I said, "Hey, Miles, pull over so I can get some shots of you and your ride." He did and I did.

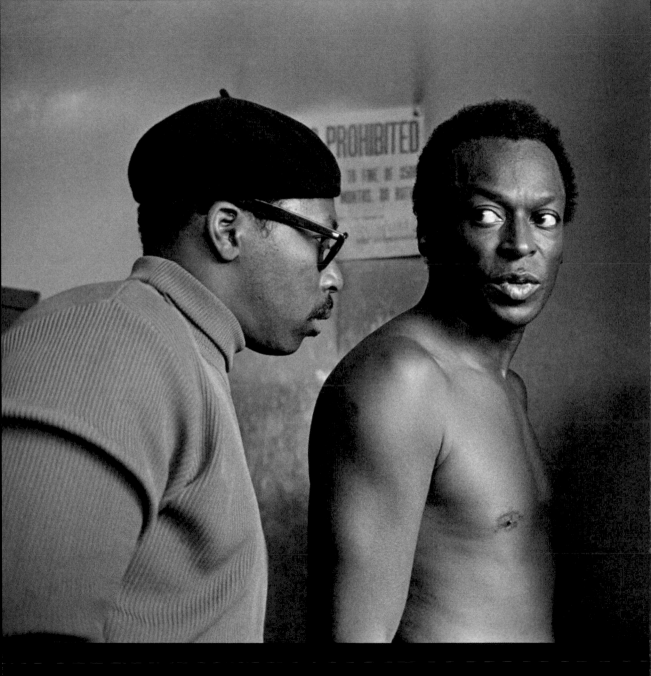

Miles Davis

1969 NEW YORK

Miles Davis weighing in and training at Gleason's
Gym in New York City, 1969. Davis loved boxing
– much has been written about how he integrated
boxing into his music and vice versa. "Don't hit me in
the mouth, I gotta play tonight," he used to say to his
training partners before they sparred.

Miles Davis

1969 NEW YORK

(*right*) Miles Davis was once asked, "If you had three wishes, what would they be?" He had only one: "I wish to be white." As the dialogue over racial inequality continues to rage in the US, I often think about Miles, a hugely talented, widely celebrated musician who did not grow up in poverty, and yet he's telling us, all of that notwithstanding, being white was his fondest, his only wish. If you're not one, there is no possible way to know what it's like to be a person of color in this country – too often a second-class citizen and a victim of prejudice simply because of the color of one's skin. Miles was working out his anger here in Gleason's gym in my 1969 photo. I'm not sure how I would handle my anger under the same circumstances.

Miles & Betty Davis

1969 NEW YORK (OVERLEAF)

Jazz great Miles Davis and his then wife, funk singer Betty Mabry Davis, in their home on the Upper West Side of Manhattan, 1969. A model and fashionista, Betty convinced Miles to dress with more flair. She also introduced him to Jimi Hendrix and Sly Stone, whose music subsequently influenced Miles' own creative directions.

Miles Davis

1969 MONTEREY

Widely considered one of the
most influential and innovative
musicians of the twentieth century,
Miles Davis was, together with his
musical groups, at the forefront
of several major developments in
jazz music, including bebop, cool
jazz, hard bop, modal jazz, third
stream, post-bop and jazz fusion.
In 2006, Davis was (posthumously)
inducted into the Rock and Roll
Hall of Fame, which recognized
him as one of the key figures in the
history of jazz. I photographed
Miles only twice, once here in
1969, at the Monterey Jazz Festival
(California), and then again later
that same year at his home in New
York City, and at Gleason's Gym
where he boxed.

Monterey Jazz Festival

1969 MONTEREY

In early 1969, my friend and fellow photographer Jim Marshall and I signed a contract to produce photos for a book to be called *Festival! The Book of American Music Celebrations*. Jim and I set out that summer to visit an eclectic mix of American music gatherings, from country and western to blues and folk, bluegrass and jazz to rock and pop. One of the highlights for me was the weekend at the annual Monterey Jazz Festival (California).

Sly Stone

1969 MONTEREY

This picture of Sly Stone, leader of the band Sly & The Family Stone, was also taken in 1969 at the Monterey Jazz Festival (California). Along with James Brown, Sly & The Family Stone were pioneers of late sixties and early seventies funk music.

Neil Young

1969 LOS ANGELES

(*right*) In June 1969, I headed over to a recording studio on La Cienega Boulevard in Hollywood on an assignment from *Rolling Stone* to photograph Neil Young. Because I hated flash I neglected to bring along a strobe of any kind. The studio was surprisingly dark and I had no light, so I ended up shooting a single roll of film at a very slow shutter speed and with the lens wide open. Neil was enormously cooperative and allowed me the freedom to shoot as he worked at the mixing board.

The Everly Brothers

1969 NEWPORT (OVERLEAF)

The Everly Brothers were American country-influenced rock and roll singers known for close harmony singing over choppy guitars, the first great pop duo of the rock era. Brothers Don and Phil were elected to the Rock and Roll Hall of Fame in 1986 as members of the very first group of inductees alongside such luminaries as Elvis, Chuck Berry, James Brown, Buddy Holly and Jerry Lee Lewis. I photographed them here in 1969 at the Newport Folk Festival. In 1957, the Everly Brothers recorded 'Bye Bye Love' which rose to number two in the pop charts and became their first million-seller. More hits followed: 'Wake Up Little Susie', 'All I Have To Do Is Dream', 'Bird Dog' and their own song, written by Don, '(Till) I Kissed You'. 'Cathy's Clown', written by Don and Phil, sold eight million copies, their biggest selling record. After a period of estrangement, the Brothers played an emotional reunion concert at London's Royal Albert Hall in 1983, and thereafter continued their performing career, including several performances with early fans Simon & Garfunkel in 2003 and 2004. Phil passed away in 2014, just days before his 75th birthday.

Albert King

1969 SAN FRANCISCO

Albert King singing the blues in San Francisco, 1969. Born Albert Nelson but better known by his stage name, King was an American blues singer and guitarist (always playing his signature Gibson 'Flying-V'), whose best-known album (and title track) was *Born Under A Bad Sign*. Because he drove a bulldozer during one of his early day jobs, and was over six feet tall and weighed 250 pounds, he was often called 'The Velvet Bulldozer'. King passed away in 1992 aged 69 and was posthumously inducted into the Rock and Roll Hall of Fame in 2013.

I was in Macon, Georgia, when I photographed Duane Allman as the group first began rehearsing as The Allman Brothers Band in the RedWal (named after partners Otis Redding and Phil Walden) Studios. Who could imagine that only a couple of years hence the extraordinarily talented Duane would leave us well before his time. Duane Allman is best known for his expressive slide guitar playing and inventive improvisational skills, and apart from the Allman Brothers records themselves is remembered for his contributions to Eric Clapton's 'Layla' album. In 2003, *Rolling Stone* ranked Allman at number two in their list of the 100 greatest guitarists of all time, second only to Jimi Hendrix.

Gregg Allman in 1969, rehearsing in Macon, Georgia, shortly after the formation of The Allman Brothers Band, when I luckily came upon them. It's fair to say that musicians pretty much all give more than they take. We have been blessed to have had the brothers Allman and their many talented fellow musical travelers in our midst for so many years, making wonderful, memorable music for us.

Blue Cheer

1969 SAN FRANCISCO

Some of us remember the San Francisco-based band Blue Cheer. Playing what was then known as psychedelic blues rock, the band was also considered to be one of the pioneers of heavy metal thanks to their 1968 cover of 'Summertime Blues'. Dickie Peterson, pictured here, was Blue Cheer's bassist and lead singer. The band came to my studio in November 1969 for an album cover shoot, from which these shots were taken. Peterson spent much of the two decades preceding his death in 2009 in Germany, where he played with Mother Ocean, a group he formed with former Blue Cheer guitarist Tony Rainier.

Plaster Casters

1969 CHICAGO

Once upon a time there were two teenage girls who were learning body casting in a Chicago art school. On one particular Friday the teacher gave them a weekend assignment: "Go out and cast something hard." And the rest is history. If you've never heard of the Plaster Casters of Chicago, the short version is that Cynthia Albritton (aka Cynthia Plastercaster) originated the idea of casting the erect private members of rock stars. The longer, more detailed, version can be found on the Internet if you're curious. At the conclusion of our 1969 photo shoot the Casters offered to cast me, a distinct honor since one must be personally invited; they don't cast just anybody. I demurred, however, suggesting they probably didn't have enough plaster with them to immortalize me in that manner...

Chuck Berry

1969 BERKELEY

Regrettably, I never photographed
Chuck Berry in performance. And
yet my 1969 informal portrait of
him at Sproul Plaza, UC Berkeley,
California, captures a joyous and
seldom-seen side of this pioneer
of rock and roll, so there is that.
Berry was an American guitarist,
singer and songwriter, and one of
the foremost innovators of rock
and roll music. With songs like
'Johnny B. Goode', 'Sweet Little
Sixteen' and 'Roll Over Beethoven',
with 'ringing a bell' guitar solos
and with his own unique brand
of showmanship, he refined and
developed rhythm and blues into
the major elements that made
rock and roll so distinctive and
compelling. In 1986, Chuck Berry
was a member of the first 'class'
to be inducted into the Rock and
Roll Hall of Fame. No musician
deserved it more.

Harvey Mandel

1969 MILL VALLEY

right) Although you should be, probably few of you are familiar with the talented guitarist Harvey Mandel, seen here in a 1969 color Polaroid photo I shot of him for the cover of his 1970 album, *Games Guitars Play*. Mandel played with Canned Heat, John Mayall, The Rolling Stones and others before heading out on a solo career. From 1968 to 2017, he appeared on twenty-five different albums.

Jann Wenner

1969 SAN FRANCISCO (OVERLEAF)

In its effort to replicate the original San Francisco office of Jann Wenner (*Rolling Stone*'s co-founder along with acclaimed music journalist Ralph Gleason), the Rock and Roll Hall of Fame kind of missed the mark. OK, they got the curved windows right as well as the dried leaves, but as you can see in my 1969 informal portrait of Jann, it overlooked some essential components, namely Jann's unique taste in interior decoration (or was it that of his wife, Jane?). The round table shown in the Hall of Fame exhibit was behind me when I took this picture; perhaps some of the other HOF accoutrements were there, too; I don't recall. Anyhow, it's more than fifty years and nearly 300 issues later, and that's all that really matters

Sonny Rollins

These are 1969 photos of Sonny Rollins playing at the Greek Theatre at the University of California in Berkeley. An American jazz tenor saxophonist, Rollins is widely recognized as one of the world's most important and influential jazz musicians, recording at least sixty albums in a seven-decade career. Noted jazz critic Stanley Crouch wrote this about Rollins in the *New Yorker*: "Over and over, decade after decade... there he is, Sonny Rollins, the saxophone colossus, playing somewhere in the world, some afternoon or some eight-o'clock somewhere, pursuing the combination of emotion, memory, thought, and aesthetic design with a command that allows him to achieve spontaneous grandiloquence." Rollins was presented with a Grammy Award for lifetime achievement in 2004. In 2006, he completed a *Down Beat* magazine readers poll triple win for Jazzman of the Year, Top Tenor Sax Player and Recording of the Year. Sadly, the now 87-year-old Sonny Rollins has not performed in public since 2012.

Nudie Cohn

1969 SAN FRANCISCO

Nudie the Tailor appeared on the cover of *Rolling Stone* issue no.36 in 1969. Nudie Cohn designed and made extraordinary (and now collectable) rhinestone-covered suits with chain-stitched embroidered themes for the stars, from Elvis to Robert Redford to Roy Rogers and beyond, including the famous suit adorned with marijuana leaves that Gram Parsons wore on the cover of The Flying Burrito Brothers album, *The Gilded Palace Of Sin*. Do yourself a favor and look him up.

James Brown

1969 SAN FRANCISCO

James Brown perpetually exhorted his audiences to be like 'a sex machine'. Lord knows, I'm tryin', James. But these days I'm pretty much a sex machine in my mind and heart only... James Brown was an American singer, songwriter, record producer, dancer and bandleader. The founding father of funk music, he's often referred to as The Godfather of Soul. I shot these in San Francisco on New Year's Eve, 1969. Brown's performances were exciting, exhilarating, electrifying, and always thrilling. We lost a super talent when James Brown died in 2006.

1970

and beyond...

Harry Nilsson

1970 LOS ANGELES

Another under-appreciated musical talent, Harry
Nilsson was a prolific American singer-songwriter
who received two Grammy awards. He achieved
considerable success with his version of 'Everybody's
Talkin'', featured in the film *Midnight Cowboy*.
I photographed him here in his Los Angeles home
in 1970. A favorite of The Beatles, Nilsson was
particularly close to John Lennon, after whose senseless
assassination in 1980 he took a break from recording
and campaigned for gun control. No stranger to
alcohol-fueled indulgence, Nilsson died from a heart
attack in 1994.

Mountain

1970 DENVER

The group Mountain, relaxed here in a band portrait I
made in Denver in 1970: (left to right) Felix Pappalardi,
Steve Knight, Leslie West, and Corky Laing. This
is my kind of group shot, much preferable to the
typical 'line 'em up and shoot 'em' PR photo. Formed
in Long Island, NY, in 1969, they were credited with
influencing the development of heavy metal music.
Their fourth concert as a working band was at the
Woodstock festival the same year but for some reason
their performance didn't appear in the film of the event.

Leslie West
& Felix Pappalardi

1970 DENVER

At the same time, I made these portraits of guitarist Leslie West (*far left*) and bass guitarist and vocalist Felix Pappalardi (*below*). Felix eventually moved on to music production and is remembered for his work with the British blues-rock power trio Cream. Sadly, in 1983, Pappalardi was shot and killed by his wife, Gail. He was 43.

West himself is an under-appreciated (in my opinion) American rock guitarist, vocalist and songwriter. Mountain (and West) played hard rock, blues rock and heavy metal. After Felix Pappalardi left Mountain to concentrate on his various production projects, West and drummer Corky Laing produced two studio albums and a live release with Cream bass-guitarist Jack Bruce under the name West, Bruce and Laing. In June, 2011, West had his lower right leg amputated due to complications from diabetes. In August, 2011, he made his first public appearance after his surgery. Johnny Ramone, a fan of West's talent, has called him "one of the five top guitar players of his era." I agree...

Devon

In 1970, I photographed Super Groupie Devon
Wilson for the premier issue of *Rags* magazine. The
shoot took place in the NYC West Village apartment
of Jimi Hendrix, Devon's man of the moment.
Decorated in contemporary Casbah, Jimi's flat
was warm and inviting. During the photo session a
considerate Jimi disappeared into the bedroom to allow
Devon her own fifteen minutes of fame. A few months
later Jimi was gone.

Creedence
Clearwater Revival

1970 SAN FRANCISCO & OAKLAND

(*above*) With his telltale plaid shirt, who else could this be but John Fogerty of Creedence Clearwater Revival, CCR. Earlier on this same day at my studio, in 1970, I shot the band for the cover of *Rolling Stone* issue no. 52. Previously called The Golliwogs, the band changed its name to CCR when John was discharged from the Army in mid-1967. A year later they really took off, releasing such classics as 'Susie Q' and 'Proud Mary', to name only two of what became a long list of hit singles. The band eventually broke up and John went solo in 1973. Legal troubles followed, as did the crooked track of John's career. I love baseball; 'Centerfield' is still my favorite song from Fogerty's later years, one that's played at ballparks around the country.

(*right*) Creedence Clearwater Revival, cover shot for *Rolling Stone* issue no. 52, San Francisco, 1970.

(*overleaf*) Before a performance most musicians can be found tuning up both their instruments and their heads. Here, backstage in the Oakland (California) Coliseum Arena in January 1970, the four members of Creedence Clearwater Revival prepare for the long walk onto the stage. Left to right: Doug Clifford, drums; Stu Cook, bassist; Tom Fogerty, rhythm guitar; and John Fogerty, lead vocalist, lead guitarist, and primary songwriter.

Creedence
Clearwater
Revival

1970 OAKLAND

John Fogerty and Creedence
Clearwater Revival headlining
a 1970 concert at the Oakland
(California) Arena, home to the
NBA's Golden State Warriors
basketball team. Rock star as
evangelist to a crowd of adoring
fans...

Betty Davis

1970 NEW YORK CITY

Betty Davis is considered one of the most influential voices of the funk era, a performer who was known for her memorable live shows. One of the first songs she ever wrote (at the age of 12!) was called 'I'm Going to Bake That Cake of Love'. She also worked as a model, appearing in photo spreads in *Seventeen*, *Ebony* and *Glamour*, and although successful was bored by the work. According to Oliver Wang's *They Say I'm Different* liner notes, she said, "I didn't like modeling because you didn't need brains to do it. It's only going to last as long as you look good." She met Miles Davis in 1967 and married him in September 1968. The marriage was short-lived due to his temperament. In just one brief year of marriage, however, she influenced him greatly by introducing him to the fashions and the new popular music trends of the era. In his autobiography, Miles credited Betty with helping to plant the seeds of his future musical explorations by introducing the trumpeter to psychedelic rock guitarist Jimi Hendrix and funk innovator Sly Stone. The Miles Davis album *Filles de Kilimanjaro* (1968) includes a song named after her and her photo on the front cover.

William Burroughs

1971 LONDON

Esquire, the elegant American and UK men's magazine, started publishing in 1933 as a quarterly, with a most respectable page size of 9½ x 13 inches. Although it also featured men's fashions, *Esquire*'s primary claim to fame was its outstanding line-up of authors, from Ernest Hemingway to F. Scott Fitzgerald and more. Nor did the magazine shy away from the so-called 'new journalism', featuring such writers as Norman Mailer, Tom Wolfe and others. I was called in to photographically honor some of its more illustrious authors for the premiere small edition. The art director gave me my marching orders: "Get them to smile!" – not an easy task with William Burroughs, photographed here in 1971 in his London flat. Burroughs was a celebrated, often dour American novelist, short story writer and essayist. Much of Burroughs' work is semi-autobiographical, primarily drawn from his experiences as a heroin addict, and he is best known for his third novel, *Naked Lunch*, a controversial work that was a subject of a court case under US sodomy laws. Beyond my work in rock and roll, this was one of my most remarkable assignments ever.

Steve Miller

1972 SAN RAFAEL (OVERLEAF)

Steve Miller tuning up backstage at the Marin Civic Auditorium, San Rafael, California, 1972. There is a woman relaxing in his dressing room. Shades of *Almost Famous*... Notice the lefty Stratocaster Steve is holding. An unconfirmed story is that two such guitars were made for Jimi Hendrix but he never picked them up so Steve bought them.

Kris Kristofferson

1972 LOS ANGELES

Kris Kristofferson starred in the 1972 cult film, *Cisco Pike*. The stellar cast included Gene Hackman, Karen Black, Harry Dean Stanton, Doug Sahm, and Viva. It's a story about a musician who turns to dealing pot when his music career falls on hard times. Here Kris takes some time away from the set in LA to relax and pick awhile.

Duke Ellington

1972 LOS ANGELES

In his dressing room with Duke
Ellington at the Ambassador
Hotel in Los Angeles, 1972.
The leader of the best known
'big band' in the history of jazz,
Ellington wrote more than
1,000 musical compositions.
Duke also won the Pulitzer
Prize for music in 1999. If you
love music as I do, it's worth
learning more about this
talented and gracious musician.

Taj Mahal

1974 BERKELEY

The Taj Mahal 'garage band'.
On a shoot for Columbia (now
Sony) Records in the seventies, I
scouted locations near Taj's home
in Berkeley, California. I wanted
an urban environmental portrait
so I posed him in front of a wall
of graffiti (art?). The kid showed
up uninvited with his 2x4 'guitar',
assumed the pose, and started
playing with Taj. A very fortunate
photo bomb. Meanwhile, check
out Taj's shoes.

Led Zeppelin

1977 OAKLAND

Robert Plant and John Bonham of Led Zeppelin at the 1977 Day On The Green concert at the Oakland Coliseum on July 24, which was, for a variety of unfortunate reasons, their last ever live show in America. Bonham passed away in 1980. Embarrassing as it is to admit, I came late to appreciate Led Zeppelin and photographed them only this one time.

Led Zeppelin

1977 OAKLAND
(THIS PAGE & OVERLEAF)

(*above, left to right*) Robert Plant, of Led Zeppelin. 'Nurses do it better…'

The guitars of Jimmy Page, or as he named the photo, 'My heavy artillery'.

John Paul Jones of Led Zeppelin with his unique triple-necked instrument: a mandolin plus six and twelve string guitars.

(*right*) Led Zeppelin's very last US concert. That weekend they played two shows for a combined audience of 110,000.

(*overleaf*) Here is a photo I shot from high in the Oakland Coliseum, the home of the baseball Oakland A's and the football Oakland Raiders. Knowing which band was headlining that day (there is a graphic clue), why are there still empty seats in the stadium? It was, indeed, Led Zeppelin. Bad blood between the band's manager Peter Grant and legendary promoter Bill Graham erupted backstage and as an indirect result Led Zeppelin never returned to the US. The 'visual hint' was that blimp-like structure that was supposed to resemble a zeppelin airship.

Jimmy Page

1977 OAKLAND

Jimmy Page at the 1977 Day On
The Green concert.

Santana

1977 OAKLAND

(*below left*) Carlos Santana, Day On The Green, Oakland, California, 1977. Santana is a Mexican-American guitarist who became famous in 1969 at Woodstock. His band pioneered a fusion of rock and Latin American music.

(*below*) Seen here with Carlos Santana at the same concert is Sheila E, singer, drummer and percussionist. Her father was the famed percussionist, Pete Escovedo, with whom she frequently performs. Sheila E and Prince joined forces during the *Purple Rain* recording sessions, and she subsequently forged a successful career in her own right.

Fleetwood Mac

1977 OAKLAND

Fleetwood Mac played at Bill Graham's iconic Day On The Green several times during the mid-seventies, and, of course, each concert featured Stevie Nicks. Her distinctive voice, mystical visual style, and symbolic lyrics were front and center at those concerts, as they have been for years during both her career with the band and as a solo artist. Nicks has received eight Grammy Award nominations, and with the band was inducted into the Rock and Roll Hall of Fame in 1998. At five feet one inch, she said she felt "a little ridiculous" standing next to Mick Fleetwood who is six feet six inches tall, so she started wearing six-inch platform boots. Nicks attributes her unique vocal and performance styles to Grace Slick and Janis Joplin, and often decorates her stage with flowers and other personal accoutrements.

AC/DC

1977 OAKLAND

Angus Young of AC/DC at one of promoter Bill Graham's fabulous Day On The Green concerts at the Oakland Coliseum in California, 1977. Until that day, AC/DC was hardly on my musical radar screen but I was blown away by the performance and have since become a big fan of the band. Ironically, it also took *Rolling Stone* itself forever to acknowledge the band's talent and widespread appeal among their fans around the world.

Dolly Parton

1978 OAKLAND

Bill Graham was creatively eclectic in the mixing of artists who performed at his superb Day On The Green concerts. Here is Dolly Parton in 1978.

Rolling Stones

1977 OAKLAND

Keith Richards is beyond ecstatic at the climactic
end of a solo at The Rolling Stones' Day On The
Green performance in July, 1978. This is one of those
wonderful peak music moments captured before the
advent of auto-focus or auto-exposure or high-speed
motor drives, and, of course, before digital. Just sayin'.

Rolling Stones

1977 OAKLAND

It was actually Mick Jagger's birthday on 26 July 1978, when I made this photo of him at one of Bill Graham's fabulous Day On The Green concerts at the Oakland Coliseum where tickets for a day of extraordinary music were a mere $12.50! Back then it was not so rare for a photographer and his/her cameras to be on stage with a major rock band like the Stones. But that was then and this is now. The best part of being up close and personal on stage with a band, in addition to getting wonderful performance shots, is the ability to visually tie the audience to the performers and in some small way illustrate the important, almost intimate, relationship between the two. Wonder who Mick is looking back at? Maybe Keith was playing off-key?

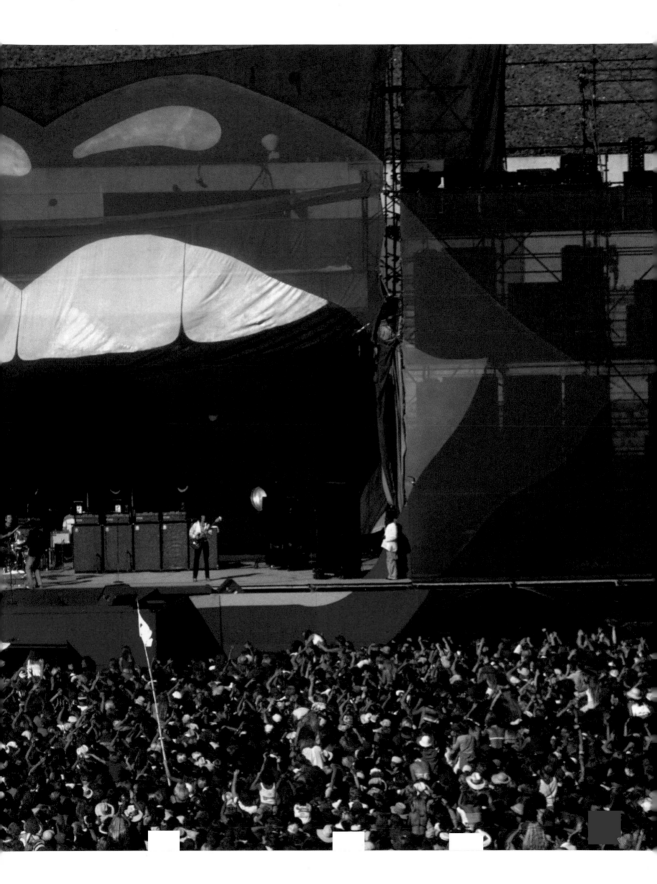

Rolling Stones

1978 OAKLAND (PREVIOUS PAGE)

Bill Graham's birthday gift to Mick and the Stones
was an amazing proscenium arch featuring the band's
famous lips visual brand. Mick is on the far left doing
the Mick dance. Keith has his back turned to the crowd
in front of Charlie. Ronnie Wood is dressed in red. Bill
Wyman is on the right. Ian Stewart is on piano. Ian
McLagan is on the Hammond. This was billed as the
Stones' Farewell Tour, since at the time it was going to
be their last. It's 2018 and they're still at it!

David Crosby

1979 BERKELEY

(*left*) David Crosby of Crosby, Stills & Nash at the
Greek Theatre, University of California Berkeley,
California, 1979. Crosby was a founding member
of both The Byrds and Crosby, Stills & Nash.
Interestingly, The Byrds gave Bob Dylan his first big
hit with 'Mr. Tambourine Man'. Neil Young joined
the group occasionally for live concerts, their second
appearance being at Woodstock, 1969.

Bootsy Collins

1979 OAKLAND

On August 4, 1979, Bill Graham presented an
offshoot of his Day On The Green concerts called
Funk On The Green #1. The lineup included
Parliament-Funkedelic, Bootsy's Rubber Band,
Brides of Frankenstein, The Bay-Kays, Sister Sledge,
Donfunkshun and Parlet. Here is Bootsy Collins and
his Rubber Band onstage.

Index

Acknowledgments

IT TAKES A VILLAGE not only to raise a child, but also to birth a book – it's a team effort. I give praise here to the entire team. To Jann Wenner who invited me to join *Rolling Stone* in 1967, and with that invitation made it possible for me to make the photos that appear on these pages.

To legendary promoter Bill Graham who gifted me with 'all access all the time', and therewith gave me an open door to the stages of his many venues, from the Fillmore Auditoriums east and west to Winterland and the amazing series of outdoor stadium concerts called 'Day On The Green.'

To Peter Beren, with whom I shared my affection for Instagram and who first suggested that a book of my Instagram classic rock photos might be of interest to fans of rock and roll, and who worked tirelessly to find a publisher who would bring his idea to fruition.

To David Barraclough, designer Lora Findlay, and the whole creative squad at Omnibus Press who magically turned the raw material into the book itself.

And to my trusted assistant, Dianne Duenzl – Dianne prepped the digital files, edited my text blocks, and provided the all-important key to the final compilation of the photo captions.

Thanks, too, to Instagram itself, the digital platform that offers photographers of the world, both professional and amateur, a global platform on which to share their personal vision through pictures – a sea change in the entire concept of photography as a means of communication.

Yes, it takes a village, and to our little community I offer sincere thanks.

Baron Wolman, Santa Fe, New Mexico, 2018